Learning to draw & drawing to learn

DRAWING The VIKINGS

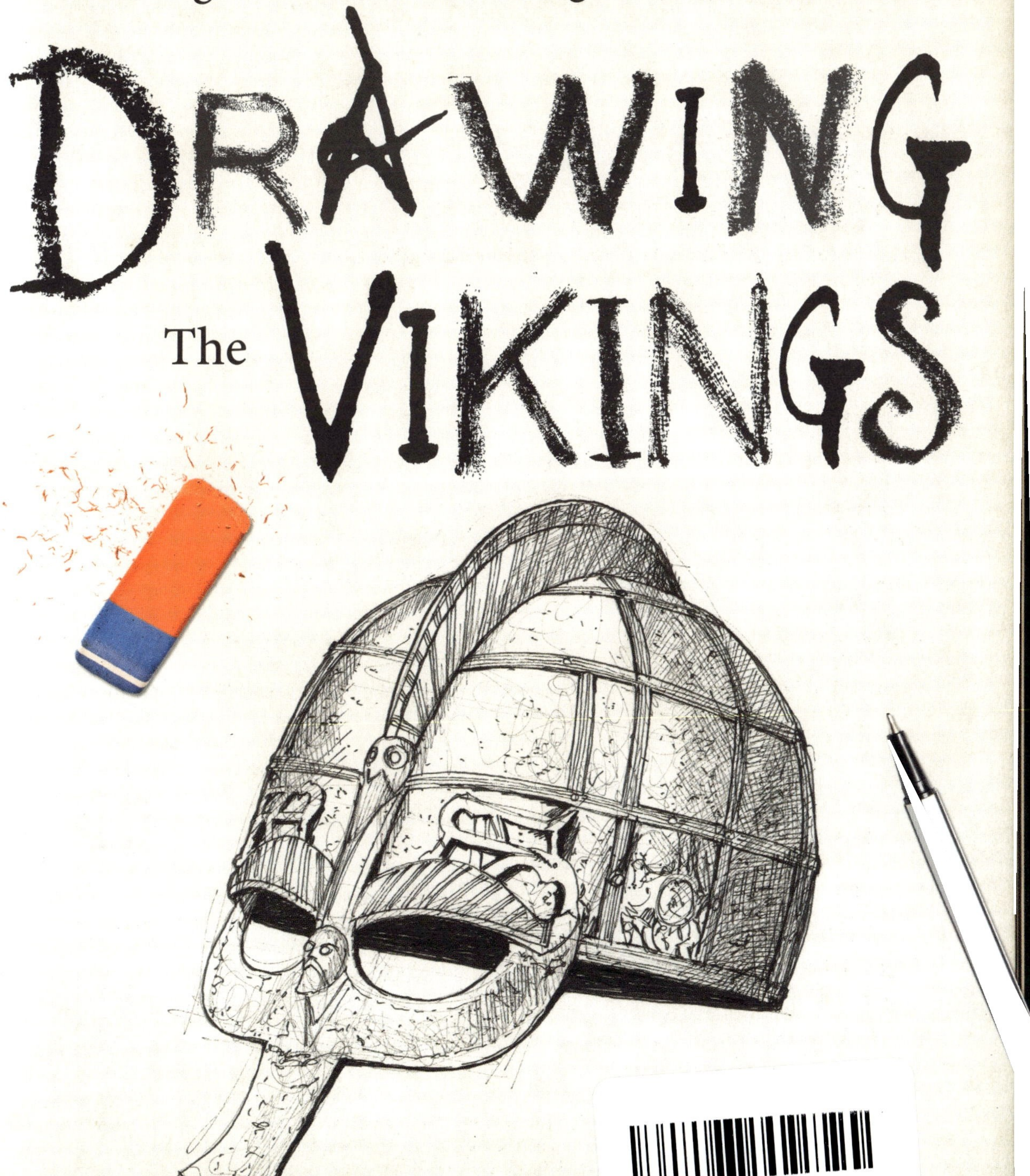

Author: Max Marlborough works as a freelance author, illustrator and designer of art guides for readers of all ages.

Artist: Mark Bergin was born in Hastings in 1961. He studied at Eastbourne College of Art and has specialised in historical reconstructions as well as aviation and maritime subjects since 1983. He lives in Bexhill-on-Sea with his wife and three children.

Editor: Nick Pierce

Photograph credits:
p4, 17, 46 Boris15/Shutterstock.com, p5, 43 severjn/Shutterstock.com, p13, 43 Mitrofanov Alexander/Shutterstock.com, p18, 46 rook76/Shutterstock.com, p31 Vitalii Khailov/Shutterstock.com, p43 Iuliia Pavlenko/Shutterstock.com, p46 Maria Luisa Cianca/Shutterstock.com, p47 gogal8128/Shutterstock.com, p50 Tatiana Dyuvbanova/Shutterstock.com, p59 RPBaiao/Shutterstock.com, p60 Taigi/Shutterstock.com

Published in Great Britain in MMXX by
Book House, an imprint of
The Salariya Book Company Ltd
25 Marlborough Place, Brighton BN1 1UB
www.salariya.com

ISBN: 978-1-912904-14-3

1 3 5 7 9 8 6 4 2

A CIP catalogue record for this book is available from the British Library.

Printed and bound in China.

Visit
www.salariya.com
for our online catalogue and
free fun stuff.

PAPER FROM
SUSTAINABLE
FORESTS

Learning to draw & drawing to learn

DRAWING The VIKINGS

Written by

MAX MARLBOROUGH

Illustrated by

MARK BERGIN

BOOK HOUSE

a SALARIYA imprint

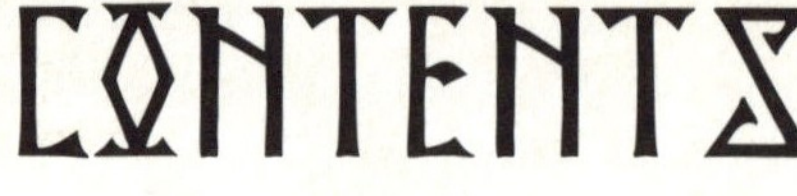

CONTENTS

40 GR
POLSKA
STATEK SKANDYNAWSKI IX W

INTRODUCTION

The Vikings were famous as marauders, explorers, traders and colonists. They lived in the Scandinavian countries in Northern Europe, and were at the height of their powers between 790–1100 AD. The Vikings were skilled craftspeople, and built ships which would take them on voyages around the coasts of Europe and across the North Sea to become the first Europeans to land in the Americas five hundred years before Columbus.

Old maps often have elaborate decorations such as sea monsters, ships and compass roses.

'Die', 'egg' and 'law' are all Viking words that we still use today. The word Viking means piracy or raiding because the Vikings had a terrifying reputation for attacking their Christian and Slav neighbours. Viking traders, raiders and settlers made their way to the Shetland Isles, the Orkneys, the Faroe Islands, Iceland, Greenland and all over Europe and beyond.

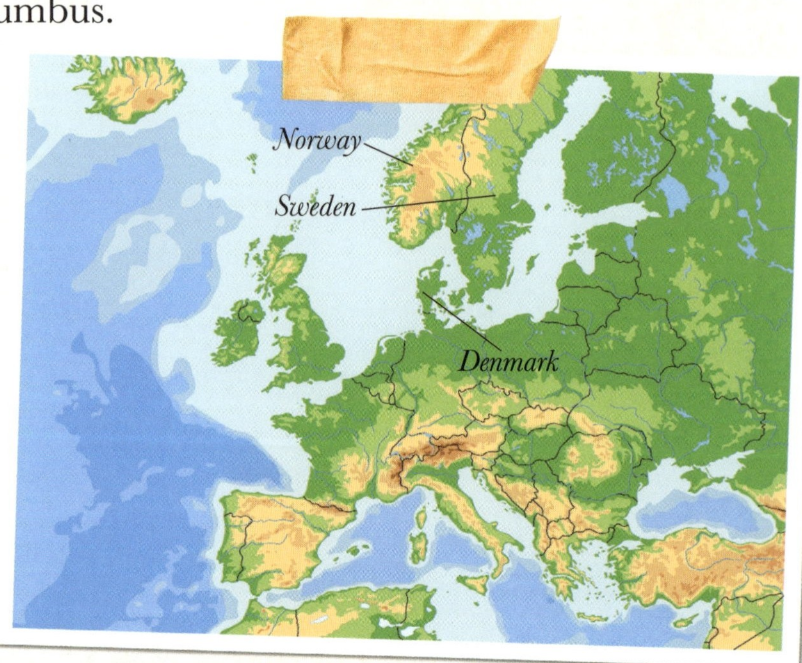

The Vikings lived in a part of the world now known as the Scandinavian countries of Norway, Sweden and Denmark.

MAKING A MAP

Copy the outlines of a map of the area.

Design small Viking icons to place on your map.

Add details to your map and a decorative border.

MATERIALS

PENCILS AND BRUSHES

Try out different grades of pencils. Brushes come in different sizes and shapes.

PAPER

Bristol paper has a good surface for crayon, pastel and felt-tip pen use. Thick watercolour paper is best for water-based paints or inks.

PAINTS

Watercolours are translucent (see-through) and gouache is opaque. Use whichever paints you prefer.

FELT-TIP PENS

Felt-tips often come in sets of mixed colours. The ones that make very thin lines are called fineliners.

STYLES

Try using different types of drawing paper and materials. Experiment with charcoal, wax crayons and pastels. All pens, from felt-tips to ballpoints, will make interesting marks, or you could try drawing with pen and ink on wet paper.

Hard pencils are greyer. They are usually graded from 6H (the hardest) through 5H, 4H, 3H and 2H to H.

Soft pencils are blacker. They are graded from B, 2B, 3B, 4B and 5B up to 6B (the softest).

Mjölnir is the hammer of Thor. Thor was the mythological god associated with thunder, lightning and storms. Thor married Sif.

Coloured pencils

Lines drawn in ink cannot be erased, so keep your ink drawings sketchy and less rigid. Don't worry about mistakes as these lines can be lost in the drawing as it develops.

Ink and wash

Silhouette is a style of drawing that uses only a solid black shape.

Felt-tips come in a range of line widths. The broader tips are good for filling in large areas of flat tone.

Ink pen
It can be tricky adding light and shade to an ink drawing. First analyse your drawing. The lightest areas should be left more or less untouched. Apply solid areas of ink to the darkest parts (the inside of the helmet). Midtones are achieved by a build up of hatching (single parallel lines) or cross-hatching (criss-crossed lines).

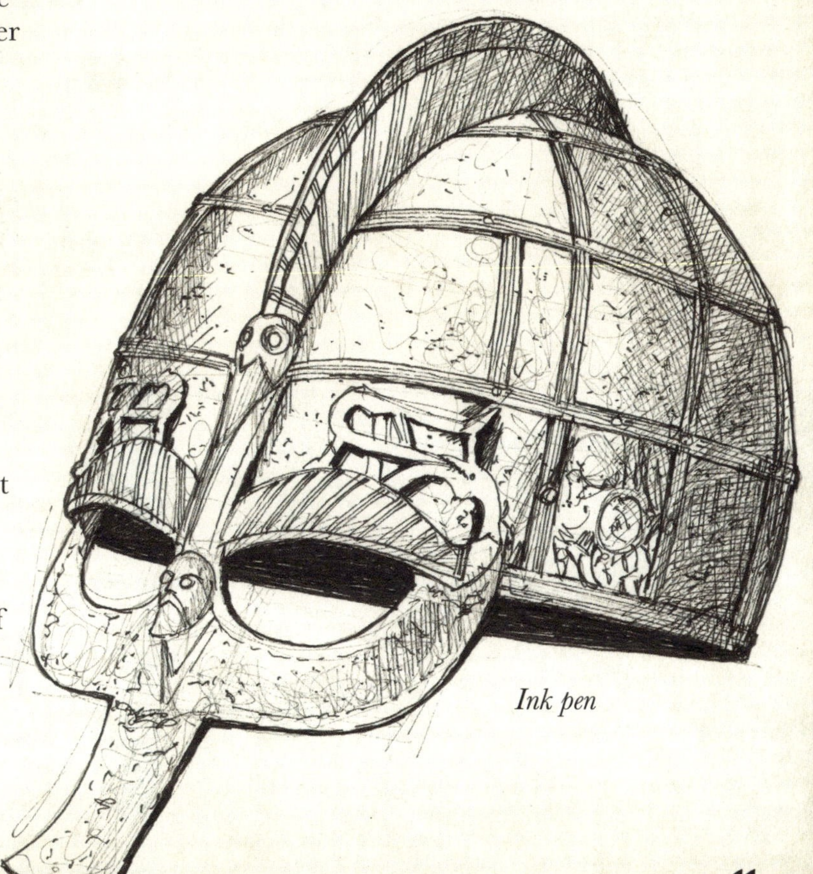

Ink pen

RUNIC ALPHABET

The symbols below spell out the name 'Leif' in Viking letters, which are called runes. Vikings did not use pens. Instead, they cut letters into wood. Runes are formed mostly of straight lines as it is hard to cut curves into wood grains. Memorial inscriptions were cut into large stones.

THE JELLING STONES

The larger of the two Jelling Stones (right) has three sides. It was raised by King Harald Bluetooth as a memorial to his parents at Jelling in Jutland, Denmark. One side is carved with runes, and pictures are carved into the other two sides.

MAGICAL POWERS

Runes were believed to have magical powers, and when carved into small pieces of wood or bone were thought to be able to tell the future. In everyday life runes were used on memorial stones and to label objects.

Runes carved in rock

Here is the Viking alphabet. UVW are all one symbol.

A B C D E F G H IJ K L M

N O P Q R S T UVW X Y Z

Jelling Stone

VIKING ART

NORTHMEN

WOLVES OF THE SEAS

The decorations found on metal and wood objects made by Viking craftsmen provide the main source of evidence of the elaborate style of Viking art.

DESIGN

The fluidity of Viking art is based on the complex interweaving of linear patterns. Curving lines swell and taper as they cross and entwine to create a wonderfully sinuous design style.

RECONSTRUCTION

The stylised lines (below) swell and taper but are always on the curve, always crossing and curling. The vitality and vigour of Viking art is clearly visible.

WOOD CARVING

The skills of the Viking artists and craftsmen are clear from the rich ornamentation they applied to everyday objects. This stave church carving is formed of gracefully stylized animal shapes interwoven within a pattern of curving lines.

Elaborately carved portal found on an exterior wall of the 12th century Urnes stave church in Norway.

FREEMAN OR SLAVE?

Viking society was divided into a hierarchy of freemen and slaves. A powerful chief was the leader of the landowners and earls who supported him. The earls themselves were supported by freemen of the neighbourhood, usually both farmers and warriors. All free Vikings knew how to handle weapons. They fought for their chief in his feuds and went with him to war. In return, the chief helped them in their disputes and rewarded them generously. When they made raids together, he shared the spoils.

A Viking chief had to be a courageous warrior and a strong leader.

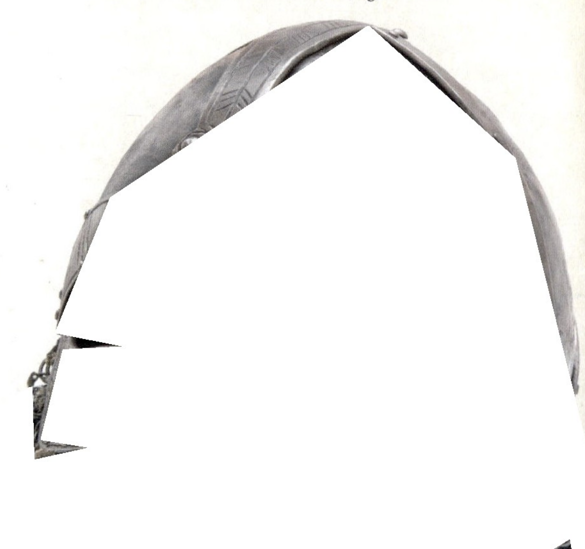

Reconstruction of a Viking helmet and chain mail. Only one Viking helmet has ever been found.

SLAVES

Slaves owned by Vikings could not own land or carry weapons. Their owner might allow them to buy their freedom with extra work. If freed, slaves could become free servants or craftsmen.

Reconstruction of burial of Viking chief with burial goods.

VIKING WARRIORS

When an earl and his men formed a raiding party, they all swore an oath to him. Each man brought his own fighting gear: sword, spear, shield, broadaxe and helmet.

Viking swords

SVERIGE

2,50

TARGETS

Monasteries were defenceless and made good targets. They provided rich pickings: holy goblets, elaborate garments, ornately jewelled boxes for storing relics or books and, of course, Christian slaves.

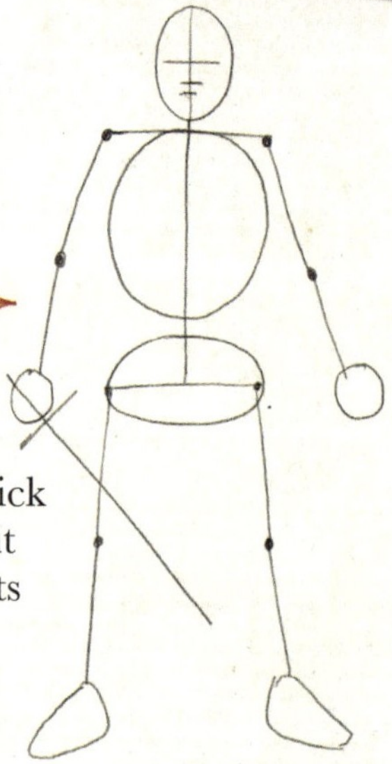

Draw a simple stick figure to work out proportions, joints and stance.

Draw a centre line. Add ovals for the head, body and hips. Mark the position of the facial features.

Join the body and hips.

Draw in the legs.

Add feet.

Draw in the shoulders, arms and hands.

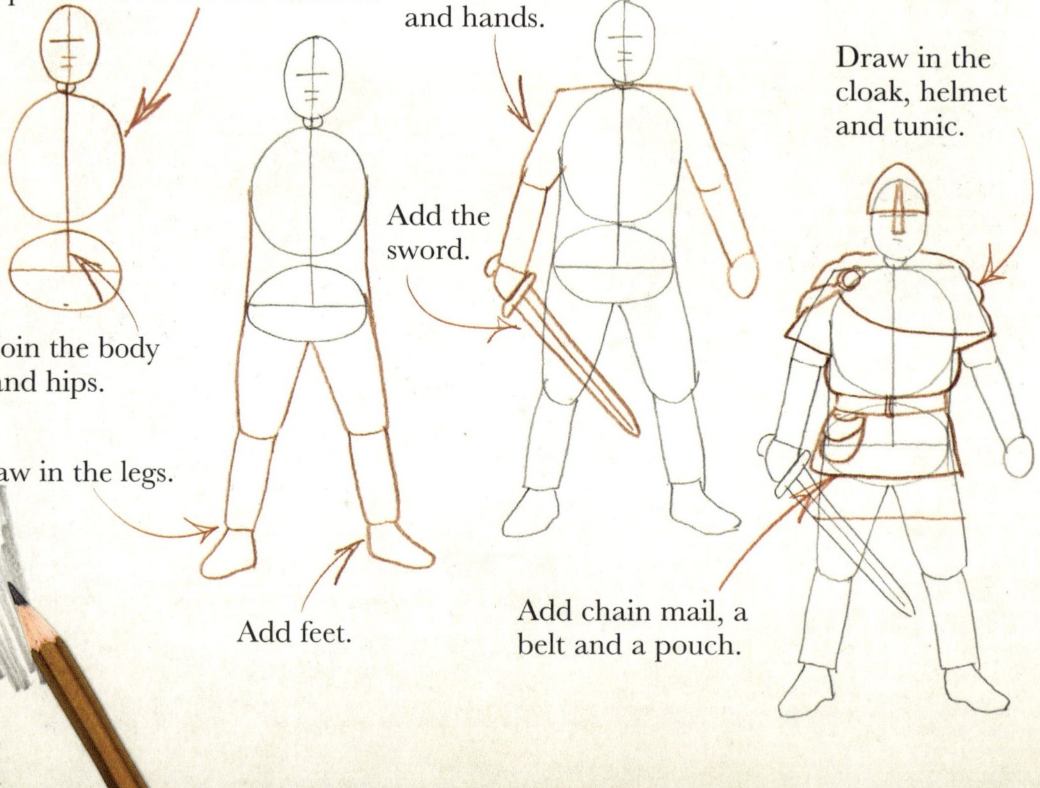

Add the sword.

Draw in the cloak, helmet and tunic.

Add chain mail, a belt and a pouch.

SHIELDS

Try different shield designs.

Erase any unwanted construction lines.

PHOTOGRAPHS

Drawing from photographs can help you to identify shape and form more accurately.

Choose a good photograph to trace.

Viking rulers had coins designed and minted as currency.

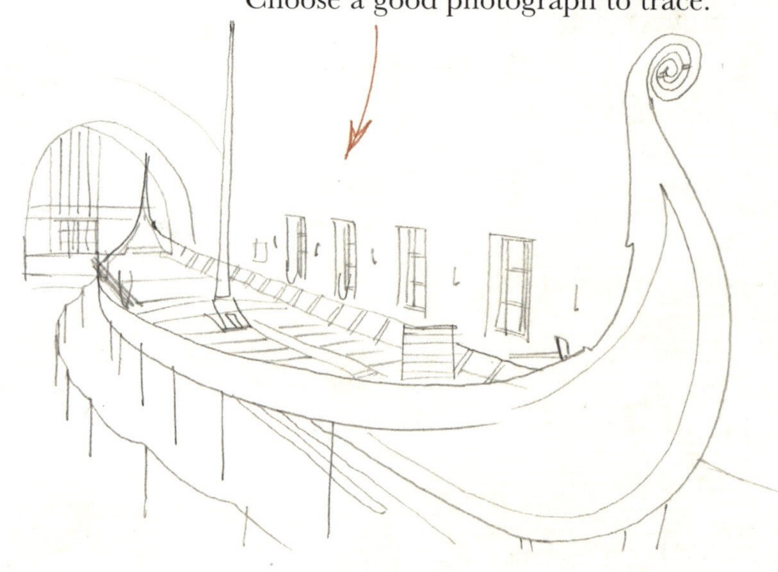

Carefully mark out a squared grid on your tracing to divide your drawing into small, equal sections.

Lightly draw a grid of the same proportions on your drawing paper. Now transfer the shapes of each square of your tracing onto your drawing paper.

Light source

Decide on your light source and add areas of shadow where light doesn't reach.

Sketch in an overall tone and add finishing details like the carved decorative touches. Erase any unwanted construction lines.

VIKING MYTHS

The early Vikings were pagans. They worshipped many gods and animals were often sacrificed to their gods at festivals. People hung their offerings to the gods on poles outside their houses. Local chiefs led worship in their own house or outside in sacred groves, or amongst the trees. The first Christian missionaries were allowed to build churches, but their bell-ringing was not popular. The Christian missionaries had only one god, but judging by the size and wealth of their churches and the stories that they told, the Vikings thought this god must be very powerful indeed. Viking merchants realised that it paid to be Christian, simply because Christians liked to trade with other Christians. Viking merchants found a compromise. Letting a priest make the sign of the cross over you made you enough of a Christian to do business with, but it was not a proper baptism, so the merchant could continue worshipping his own gods if he wanted.

The Vikings enjoyed hearing fireside stories about their pagan gods in old songs, or listening to skalds reciting and singing about them. A skald was a Viking chief's professional poet. His job was to entertain at feasts and to proclaim his employer's brave deeds in verse, so that he would never be forgotten. A skald would also have recited verses about the great god Odin's realm of Gladsheim, where he rode an eight-legged horse called Sleipnir, or told of Thor's mighty hammer, or of Sigurd the dragon slayer and many other tales. Fierce female spirits called Valkyries hovered over the battlefields and took the slain to Asgard, where they were welcomed with horns filled with ale.

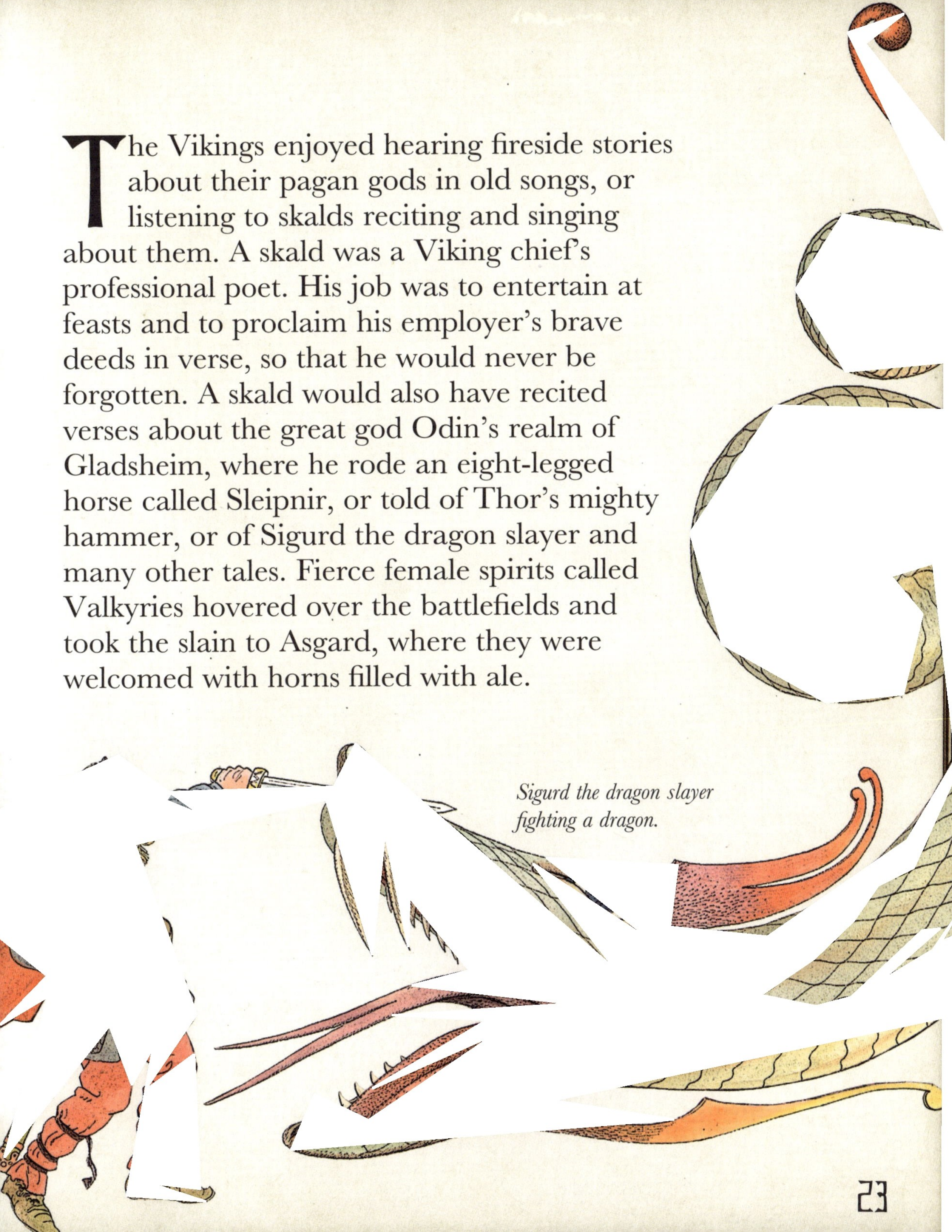

Sigurd the dragon slayer fighting a dragon.

VIKING GODS

There were many gods in the Viking mythology, each with different powers and personalities, from the heroic Thor to the mischievous trickster Loki.

Draw a simple, jointed stick figure holding a spear.

Draw in the arms, legs and body.

Add an eyepatch and hair.

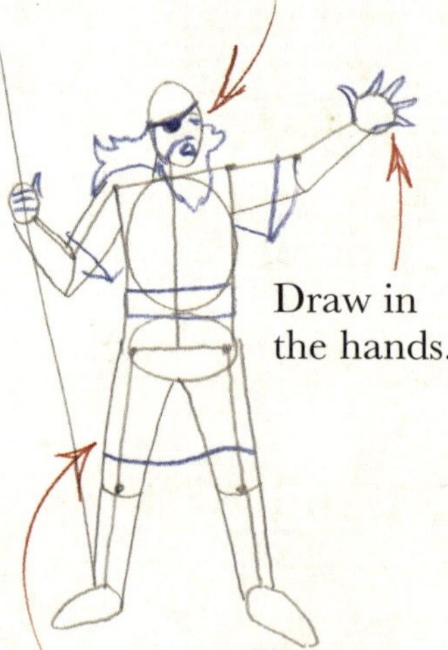

Draw in the tunic.

Erase any unwanted construction lines.

Odin
Thor
Freya
Hermod
Frigg
Tyr
Loki
Heimdall
Sigurd
Hel

SAGAS

Sagas are like historical fiction. They are based on historical characters and events, which saga writers have made into poetic stories. However, as the real events took place hundreds of years before the sagas were written, they cannot be considered as true history.

ODIN

The mysterious god Odin gave the gift of poetry and the magic of runes to the world. He lost an eye in his search for wisdom. Frigg, Odin's wife, has her own palace where she sits spinning thread to weave into clouds. The trickster god Loki often changed shape. When he was a mare, he gave birth to Odin's eight-legged horse. Balder, Odin's son, who was loved by all the gods, was killed by a spear of mistletoe, through a trick played by the evil god Loki.

THE VALKYRIE

In Viking mythology, fierce female Valkyries rode into the battlefields to take the slain back to Asgard.

THE THREE NORNS

The Three Norns of the Viking sagas are goddesses who spin the thread of life and death. They are like the Fates in Greek mythology, controlling each human's destiny.

MYTHS AND LEGENDS

Through the long, dark winter nights, people huddled around the fireside to listen to stories about kings, gods, beautiful women, dangerous journeys and terrifying fire-breathing dragons that guarded vast treasures. These stories were not written down. They were kept alive for centuries through constant retelling by storytellers called skalds.

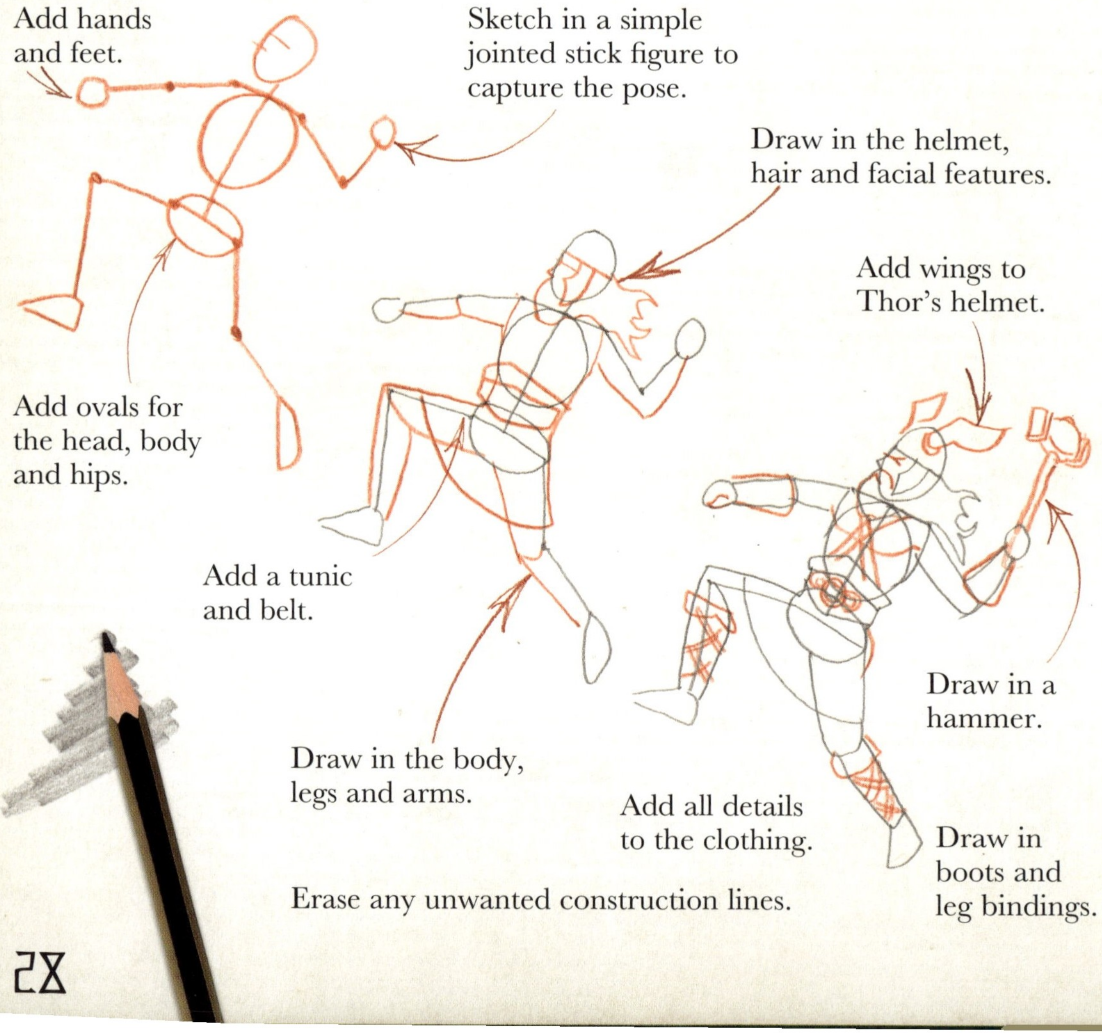

Add hands and feet.

Sketch in a simple jointed stick figure to capture the pose.

Draw in the helmet, hair and facial features.

Add ovals for the head, body and hips.

Add wings to Thor's helmet.

Add a tunic and belt.

Draw in a hammer.

Draw in the body, legs and arms.

Add all details to the clothing.

Draw in boots and leg bindings.

Erase any unwanted construction lines.

THE WORLD SERPENT

Jörmungandr, a serpent, was one of Loki's three children. Odin tossed Jörmungandr into the ocean where the serpent grew big enough to surround the Earth by grasping its own tail. It became known as Midgard, the World Serpent.

Look at old artwork for ideas for your serpent.

Thor battling Midgard, the World Serpent.

CLOTHING

For most of the year the Vikings needed really warm clothing to cope with the snow, wind and rain of the Scandinavian climate, at home or at sea. Women had to fetch water, chop wood, herd animals and do many other outdoor jobs. Clothes were almost always made at home by the women of the family or their servants or slaves. Sheep were kept to provide wool to make warm cloth. This, however, was a lengthy process.

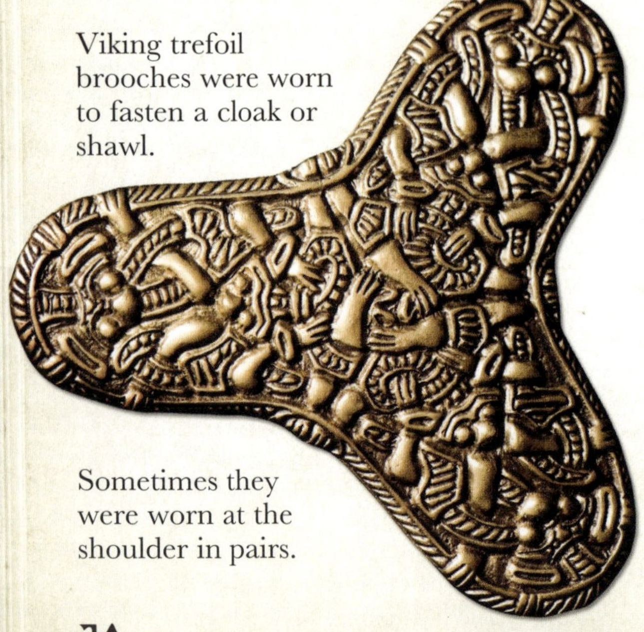

Viking trefoil brooches were worn to fasten a cloak or shawl.

Sometimes they were worn at the shoulder in pairs.

A pendant depicting Mjölnir, the hammer of Thor.

Clay loom weights like these were used to keep the warp threads taut for weaving.

VIKING WOMEN

Viking women were skilful weavers. They spun wool into yarn and used natural plant dyes to give it colour. Markets in large towns sold silks from the Far East as well as expensive fine wool cloth imported from Frisia (a coastal region along the south-eastern corner of the North Sea in what today is mostly part of the Netherlands). The tough fibres of the flax plant were woven into linen for underclothes. The flax had to be beaten to make the fibres fit for use. Animal skins provided waterproof protection and animal furs provided real warmth.

JEWELLERY

The style of jewellery worn by men and women usually featured animals. Viking rings, brooches, bracelets and necklaces were designed to show status. The jewellery was made from a variety of precious and more everyday materials: gold, silver, bronze, pewter and animal bones. Men usually wore a single brooch on their right shoulder, and women wore one on either shoulder to fasten their shawls.

BROOCH

Start with the basic pin and head.

Wealthy Vikings favoured jewellery made from bronze and silver. The most popular designs were inspired by nature and Norse mythology. Ordinary people would wear beads made of carved horn, bone or iron.

Add a decorative circular clasp.

Draw in all details.

Add tone to create the metal's sleek and 3D effect.

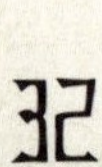

BRACELET

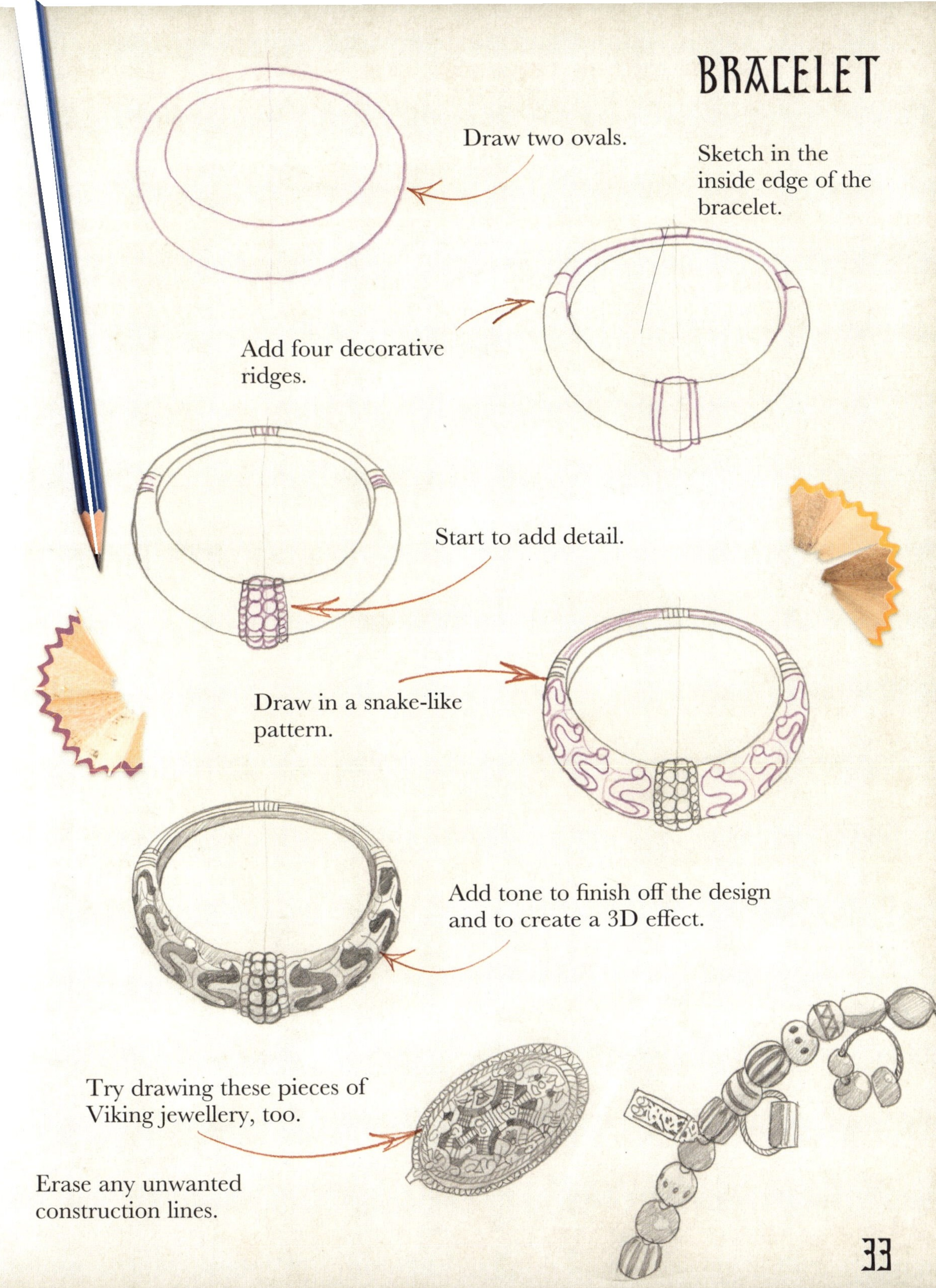
Draw two ovals.
Sketch in the inside edge of the bracelet.
Add four decorative ridges.
Start to add detail.
Draw in a snake-like pattern.
Add tone to finish off the design and to create a 3D effect.
Try drawing these pieces of Viking jewellery, too.
Erase any unwanted construction lines.

RAIDERS

Vikings often carried out raiding parties in Christian lands. The people of these lands were wealthy, with plenty of gold, silver and fine furnishings in their houses, which could easily be taken from them in a surprise attack. Monasteries were good defenseless targets that provided rich pickings – holy goblets, and richly jewelled boxes for relics.

Encampments in the Anglo-Saxon and Frankish lands were set up so that raids could be launched from a fixed base. A strong leader could take over large areas of land, which would provide good farming for Viking settlers.

KEEPING CLEAN

The Anglo-Saxons described the Vikings who attacked them as being very clean, because they would bathe once a week. At this time, an Anglo-Saxon might only bathe once or twice a year. The original meaning of the Norse words for Saturday (laugardagur, lördag, lørdag) was 'Washing Day'. Personal grooming items like combs, razors, tweezers and ear-spoons (for removing earwax) are some of the most common items found in Viking burials. Vikings made soap with a high quantity of 'lye' in it, which was used not only for bathing but also for bleaching their hair as blond hair was highly admired, and thought to be a deterrent to lice.

The Vikings were regular bathers, as evidenced by baths built in the Norse era which still exist in Iceland today. At Reykholt, Snorri Sturluson built a bath that was fed from the hot springs with steps leading down into it. The Vikings bathed in the warm, relaxing waters of the hot springs as a social activity, but women came too, to wash clothes there.

FIGURES IN ACTION

The Vikings were traders, raiders, farmers, shipbuilders and craftworkers. Day-to-day life was always physically demanding, whether it involved ferocious raiding or simply chopping wood, cooking, building or drawing water.

Draw simple jointed stick figures. Add ovals for the head, body and hips.

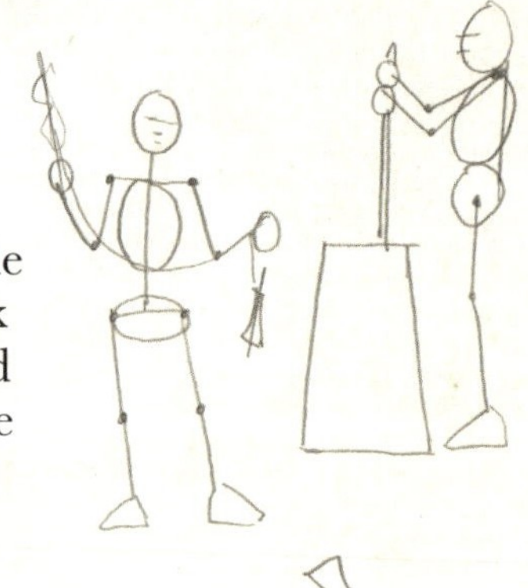

Simple stick figures help to capture body stance and movement.

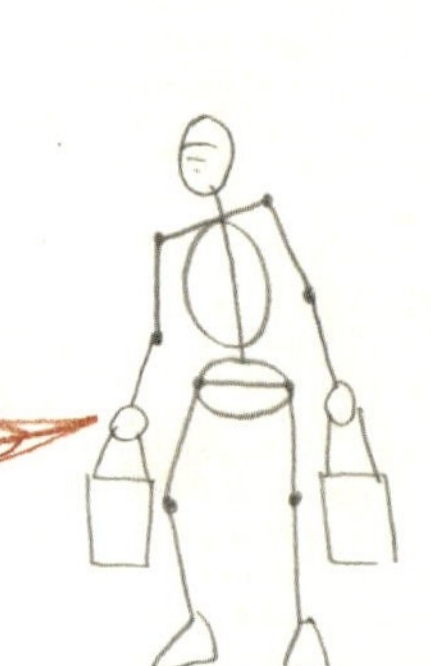

Start by adding the arms and legs.

Sketch in tools or equipment.

Add clothing.

Add all finishing details.

Add the axe head
and the shield.
Draw a simple
stick figure holding
an axe shaft.
Draw in the
body, arms
and legs.
Add the shape
of the tunic.
Draw in the helmet,
hair and facial details.
Complete all
final details.
Sketch in
the chain
mail.
Add detail
to shield.
Add the cape
and the belt.
Draw in the boots
and leg bindings.
Add tone and shading
to areas light would
not reach.
Erase any unwanted
construction lines.

VIKING VILLAGERS

Most Vikings lived in small farms, villages or hamlets. Villagers had to be self-sufficient so all their needs relied on what they grew or made themselves. They kept cows, goats and pigs and grew hay and barley. Sheep were also kept so their fleece could be made into warm clothing.

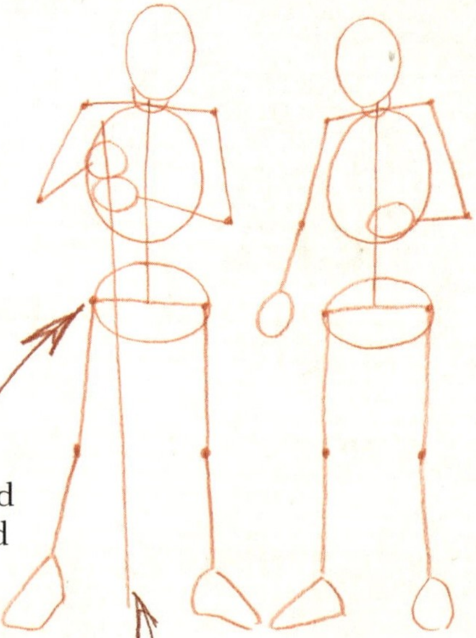

Draw two jointed stick figures. Add ovals for the body, head and hips. Add simple shapes for the feet and hands.

Draw a line for the staff.

Draw her dress and apron.

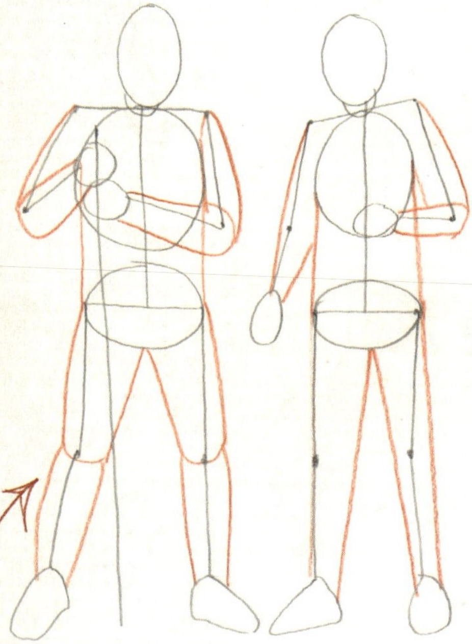

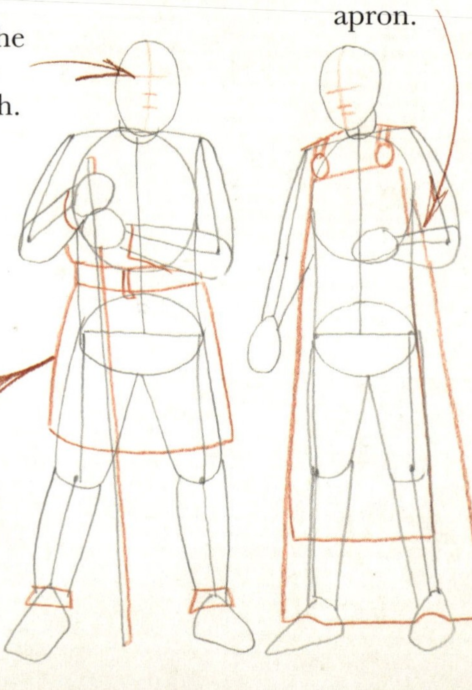

Indicate the eyes, nose and mouth.

Sketch in the body shape. arms and legs.

Draw in a belted tunic and trousers.

Draw in the faces.
Add hat.
Add scarf.
Draw hands holding a wooden plate and a jug.
Add detail to all the clothing.
Divide the apron into sections.
Add a pouch and a small knife.
Viking clothing was generally loose and simple.
Add patterns to clothing and complete all the final details.
Add shading to create form and darker shading where light does not reach.
Add two children to the family.
Erase any unwanted construction lines.

VIKING SHIPS

The Vikings were expert shipbuilders and seamen. They were famous throughout the northern seas for building ships which were exceptionally swift, yet strong enough to withstand the battering of winds and ocean waves. Viking communities were usually settled along rivers and inlets so ships had to be flat enough to travel far inland along rivers.

The Vikings built a variety of boats for fishing, as well as ferries and boats for sailing up inland rivers and lakes. These smaller boats were intended to move cargo upstream to settlements and villages.

The Vikings used a variety of ship designs for different purposes. Long, shallow ships were used for raiding and warfare. Wider merchant vessels were designed for trade and transport. Such ships would have carried settlers west to the islands in the North Atlantic.

The Oseberg Ship is a well-preserved clinker built Viking ship that was interred in a large burial mound at Oseberg, in Norway, around AD 834. The ship, which was excavated in 1904–1905 is thought to be even older. It is 22 m (71 ft) long and almost 6 m (16.7 ft) wide. It is now housed in the Viking Ship Museum on the Bygdøy peninsula in Oslo.

VIKING LONGSHIP

Viking longships had a shallow draft which made these sleek ships into deadly weapons of war. They could be landed easily or sailed up river to make surprise raids. Powered by sail and oars, they were fast inland.

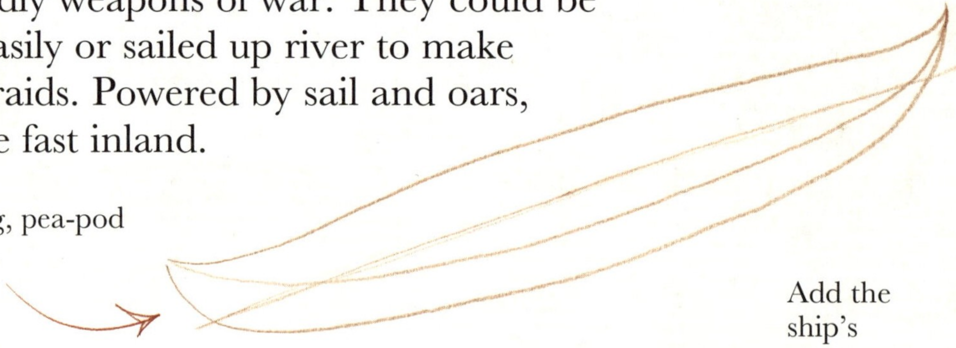

Draw a long, pea-pod shaped hull.

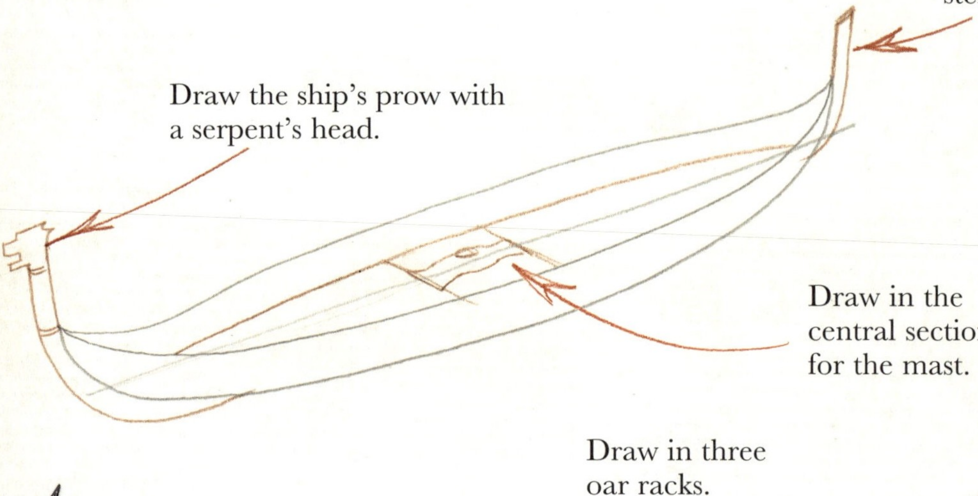

Add the ship's stern.

Draw the ship's prow with a serpent's head.

Draw in the central section for the mast.

Draw in three oar racks.

Sketch in lots of small circular shields.

Add lines for the oars.

Add a small flag.
Draw in the mast.
Add the sail.
Draw in ropes to connect the sail to the boat.
Add stripes to the sail.
Add shading to the water.
Draw in all final details.
Add Vikings to the boat.
Draw in the wooden planks of the hull.
Erase any unwanted construction lines.

SHIP DECORATION

Ships were a symbol of Viking power, which took them to war, to distant countries and sometimes to the grave. Some Vikings were buried with their ship or set alight in it. Skilled Viking shipbuilders would keep their eyes on growing trees to spot the shapes that were required for certain parts of a new ship.

The prow and stern of the Oseberg Ship are richly carved with beautiful animal patterns which start below the waterline and go all along the prow to become a carved serpent's head.

Model of a Viking ship

The Vikings' innovative methods of shipbuilding gave them the superiority they needed. Viking longships were extremely swift. They were strong enough to cross the Atlantic, yet light enough to be rolled across country on logs and make beach landings easy. Vikings raided, traded and conquered all over Europe and as far as Russia.

One of five beautifully-carved wooden animal heads that were found in the Oseberg burial mound.

VIKING SHIP DETAILS

All ships built by the Vikings, whether large or small, had certain common features. They were all 'clinker built', which meant their hulls were made of overlapping planks of wood which were riveted together with iron rivets. They used caulking to fill the gaps between the planks to make the ships watertight.

Rudder

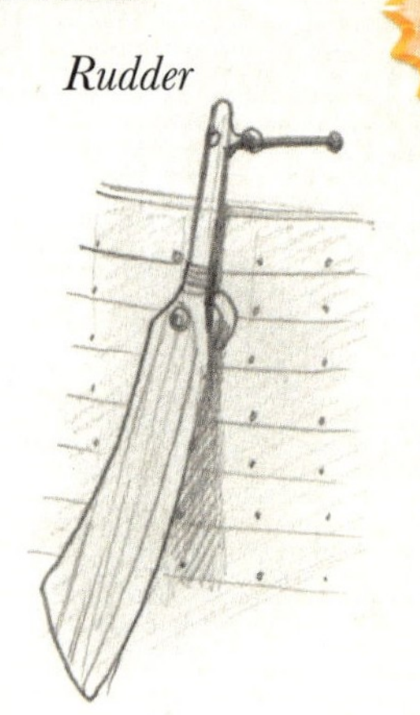

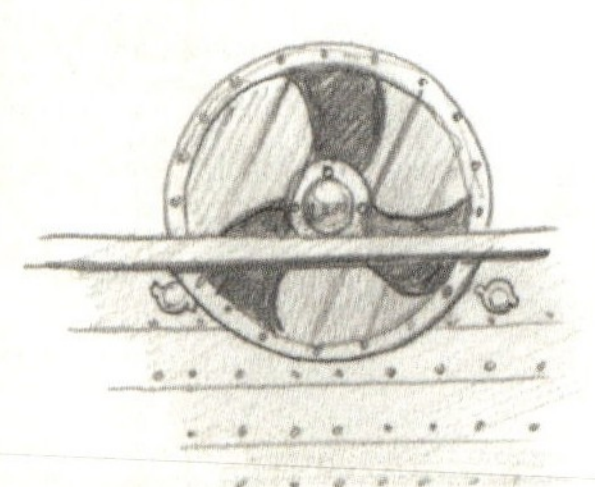

The shield rail runs along the side of the ship.

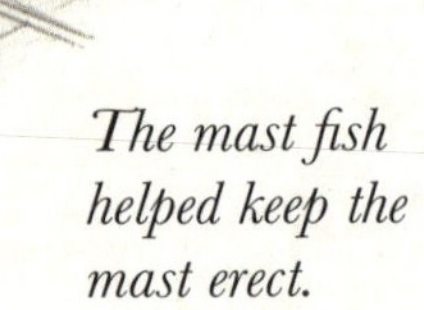

The mast fish helped keep the mast erect.

SERPENT FIGUREHEAD

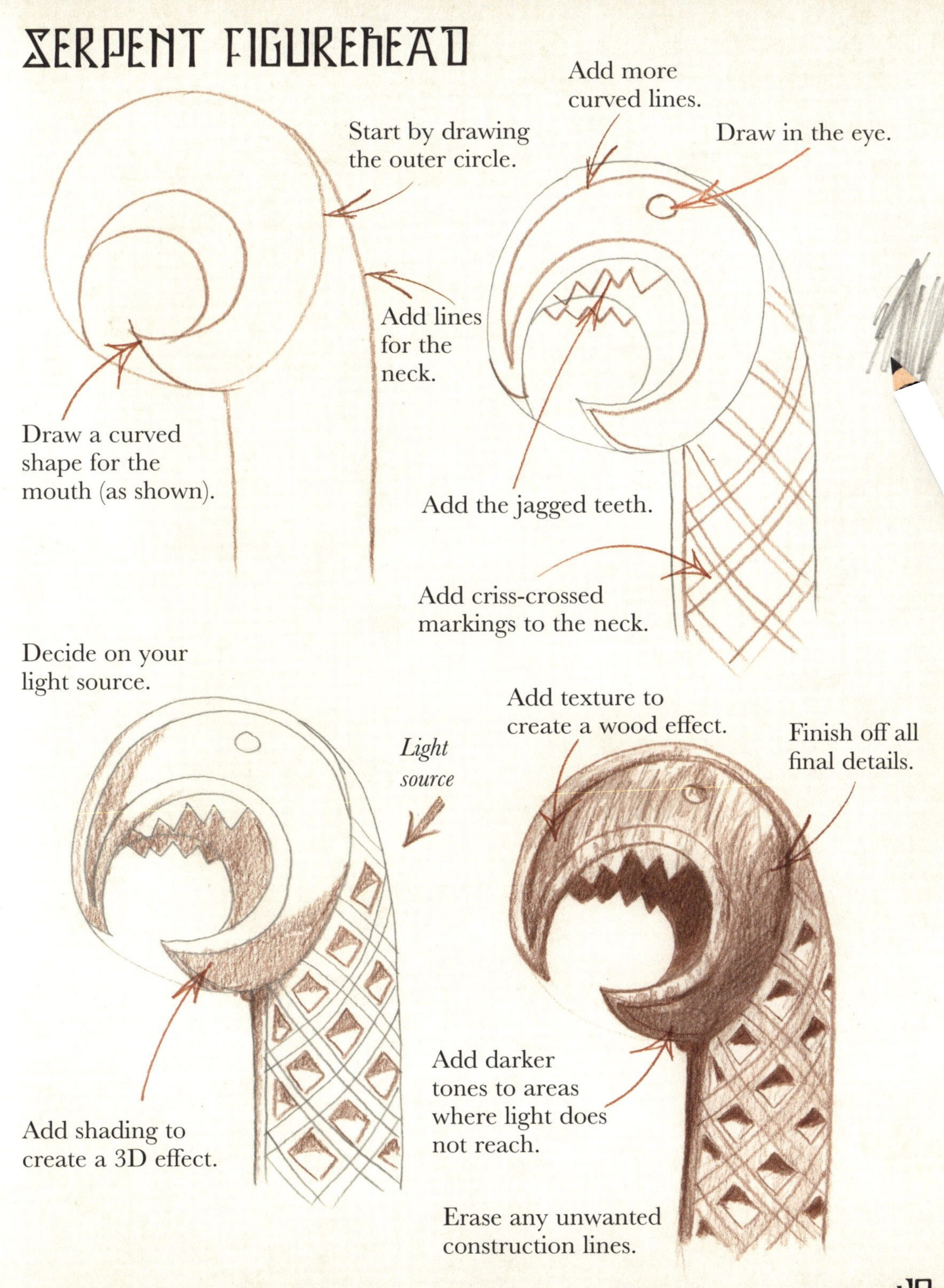

VIKING HOUSES

Viking longhouses were generally built of wood, although stone and peat were used, especially in Norway. In Iceland, Greenland and the Faroe Islands they were mostly built of stone and peat as wood was scarce. Nothing now remains of the wooden longhouses, but archaeological evidence from some sites shows how they might have looked and also what might have been found inside.

Interior of a Viking longhouse.

Longhouse roofs were often made of thatch or wooden shingles. Some had moss and grasses growing wild on the roof.

Longhouses sometimes had slightly curved walls and could range in length from nearly 50 m (164 feet) to 83 m (272 feet). Viking homes were rarely more than 5 m (16.4 feet) wide, hence the term 'longhouses'. Benches were used for seating and for sleeping – they were hung on walls when not in use. Wooden chests, used for storing jewellery, silver and clothing, were also used as seats.

PERSPECTIVE

If you look at anything from different viewpoints, you will see that the part that is closest to you looks larger, and the part furthest from you looks smaller. Drawing in perspective is a way of creating a feeling of depth – of showing three dimensions on a flat surface.

Single-point perspective uses one vanishing point (V.P.): a single reference point where lines converge to create a sense of background and foreground.

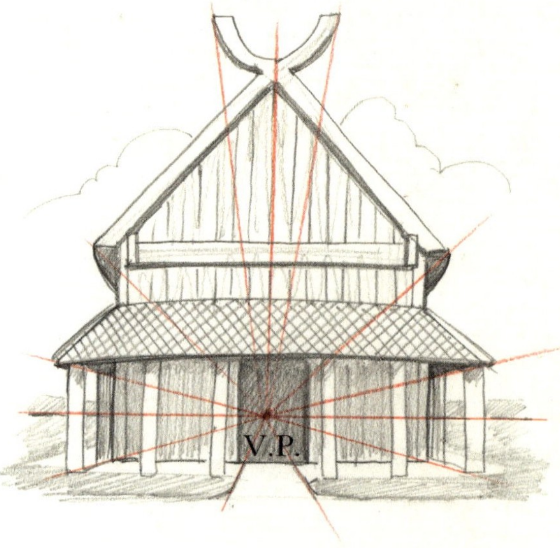

V.P. = vanishing point

Two-point perspective uses two vanishing points: one for lines running along the object and one on the opposite side for lines running across the object.

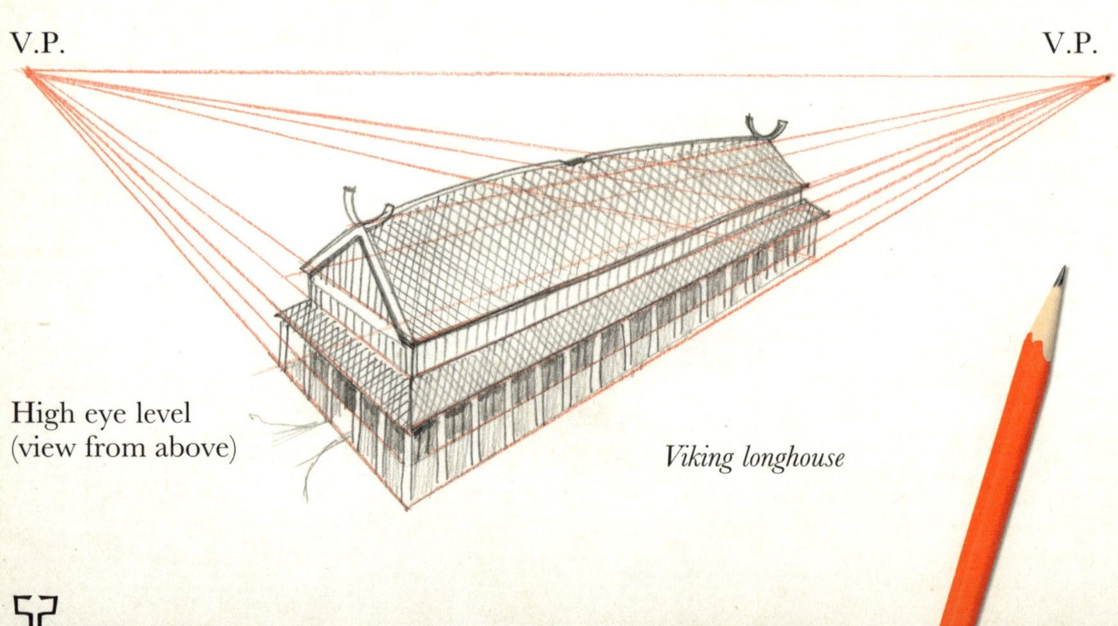

Viking longhouse

The vanishing point (V.P.) is the place in a perspective drawing where parallel lines appear to meet. The position of the vanishing point depends on the viewer's eye level. Sometimes an unusually high or low viewpoint can give your drawing added drama.

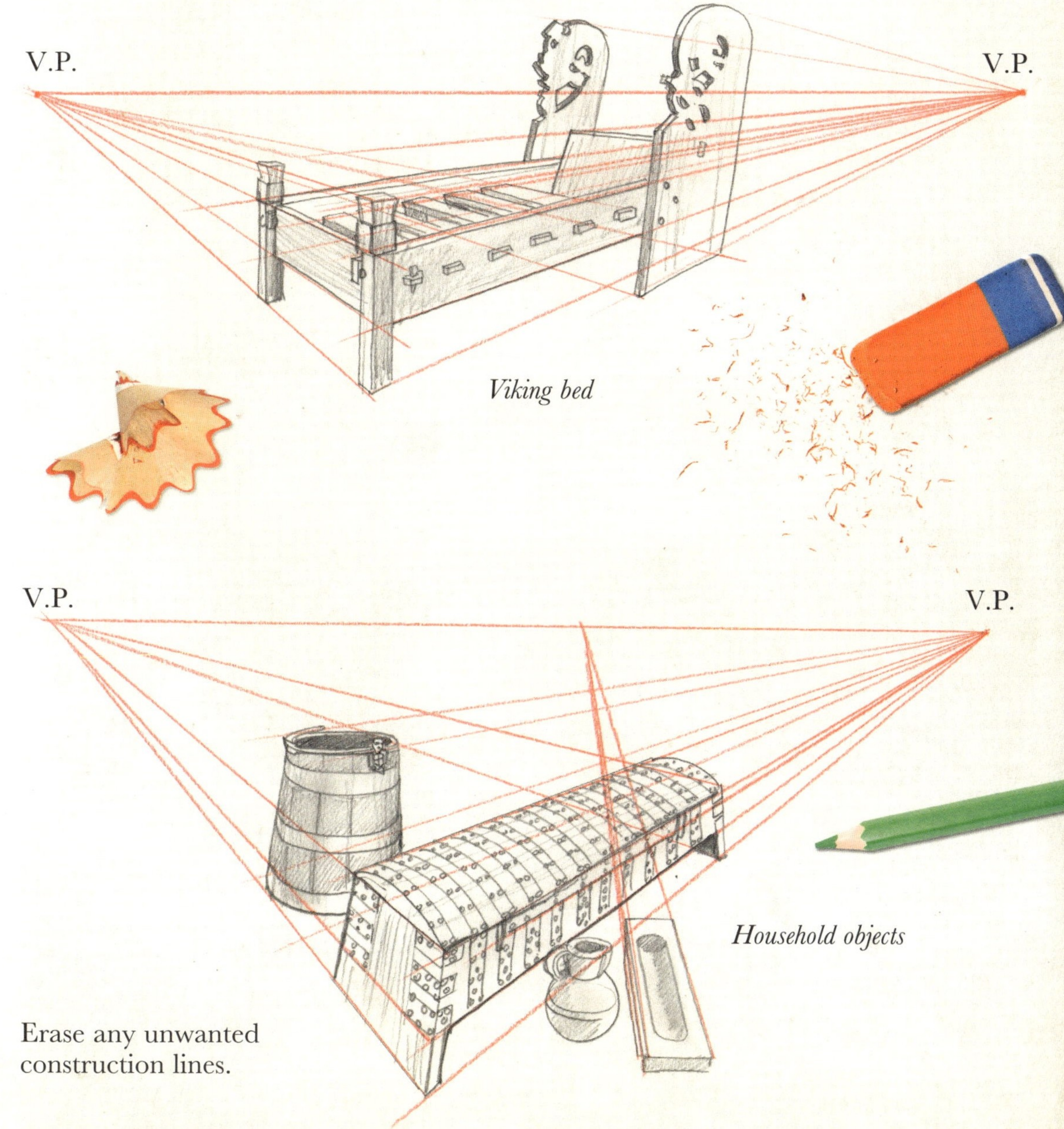

Viking bed

Household objects

Erase any unwanted construction lines.

HOARDS

A hoard is an archaeological term for a collection of valuable objects which may have been buried in the ground on purpose. Hoards do not seem to have been buried in houses, but on top of burial sites and roads. Some hoards were given a very shallow burial. The hoards were not meant to be dug up; they may have been a sacrifice to the gods to make sure of a good harvest, good health or a safe journey.

On their voyages, the Vikings are known to have traded in a wide range of goods like furs, beeswax, honey, salt and iron. Such goods would have been obtained through a combination of trade and raiding. These items, however, don't account for the rich hoards discovered by archaeologists. It is thought that much of the Vikings' lucrative trading may have come from selling slaves.

Viking traders who settled in England began to make and use coins of their own.

DRAWING MUSEUM OBJECTS

Many Viking artefacts recovered from hoards or burial mounds can be viewed in museum collections. If a museum near you has a Viking collection, it's worth visiting so you can see objects close up and draw them on site.

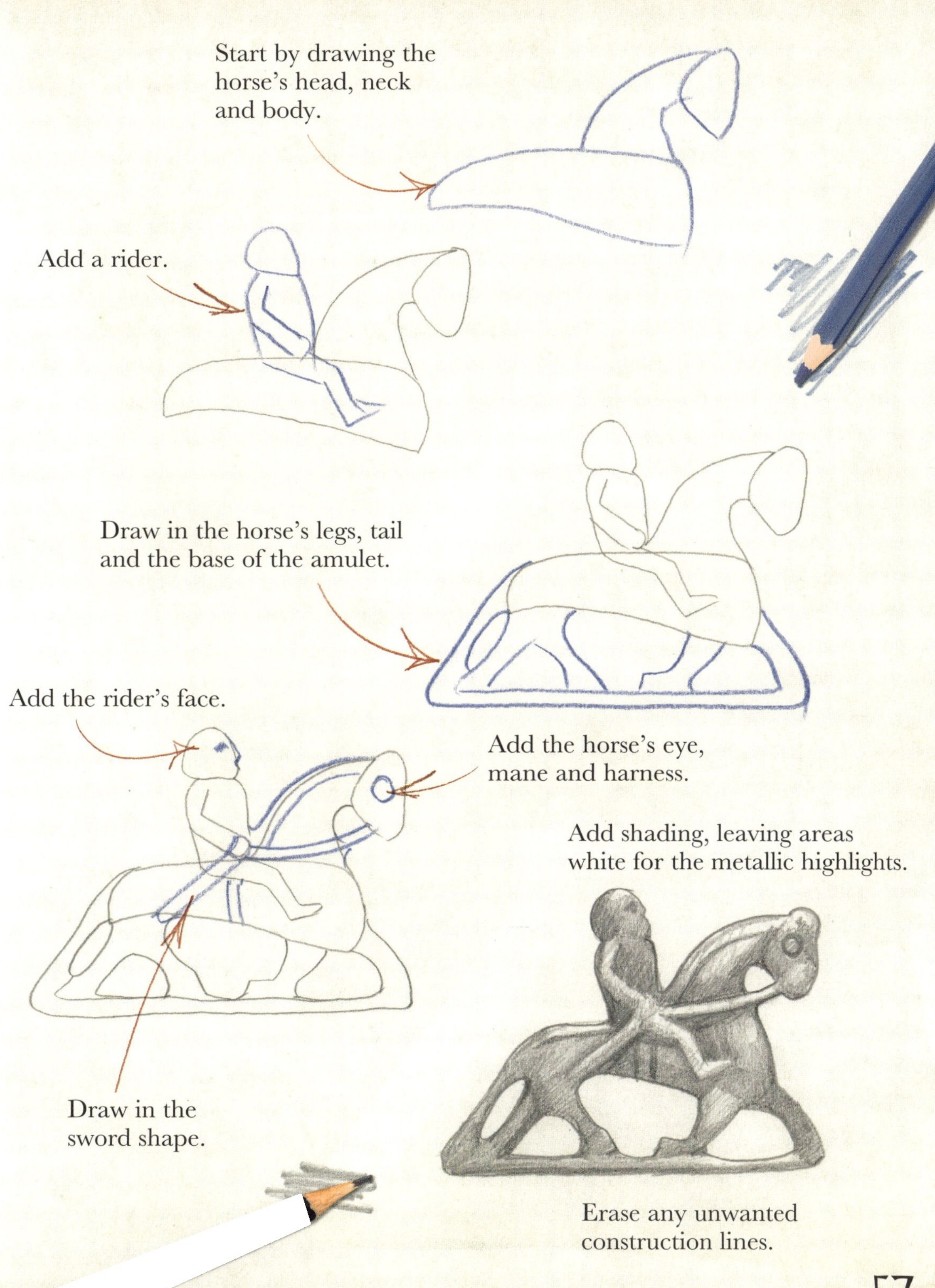
Start by drawing the horse's head, neck and body.
Add a rider.
Draw in the horse's legs, tail and the base of the amulet.
Add the rider's face.
Add the horse's eye, mane and harness.
Add shading, leaving areas white for the metallic highlights.
Draw in the sword shape.
Erase any unwanted construction lines.

STAVE CHURCH IN NORWAY

Christianity was slowly introduced into Norway. However, the Norse sagas tell of 'killings and blunt force' being used to make these conversions.

In 1020, the Old Norse pagan beliefs were finally abolished and Christianity was introduced as the official religion of Norway by King Olaf Haraldsson (born 995–died 1030).

All traces of decorations associated with the 'pagan' practices were removed from the 'heathen hofs', or existing halls of worship (in Old Norse a hof is a hall). Building new churches would have been time-consuming, so existing pagan hof buildings were adapted to be reused as Christian churches as a practical, quick and inexpensive solution.

The main reason why the Norwegian Christian kings introduced the new religion was that it recognised royal authority. The King was the head of the Church so Christianity was a useful tool for defeating opposition from Viking earls and chieftains, and thereby weakening their power.

Old Norse hofs, built alongside fjords and rivers where people travelled, were highly visible.

They were easily converted into churches by removing all traces of wood or stone and by forcing priests (hofgoði) and priestesses (hofgyðja) to convert.

Heddal Stave Church, the largest stave church in Norway.

STAVE CHURCH

In the Middle Ages, there were more than 1,000 stave churches in Norway. Today, only 28 remain. A stave church is made of wood – 'staver' means 'staves' in Norwegian.

DRAWING STAVE CHURCHES

The distinctive tiered shape of stave churches is constructed out of timber. Most of the surviving stave churches are found in Norway, where 28 still remain standing. These date from around 1150–1350 AD.

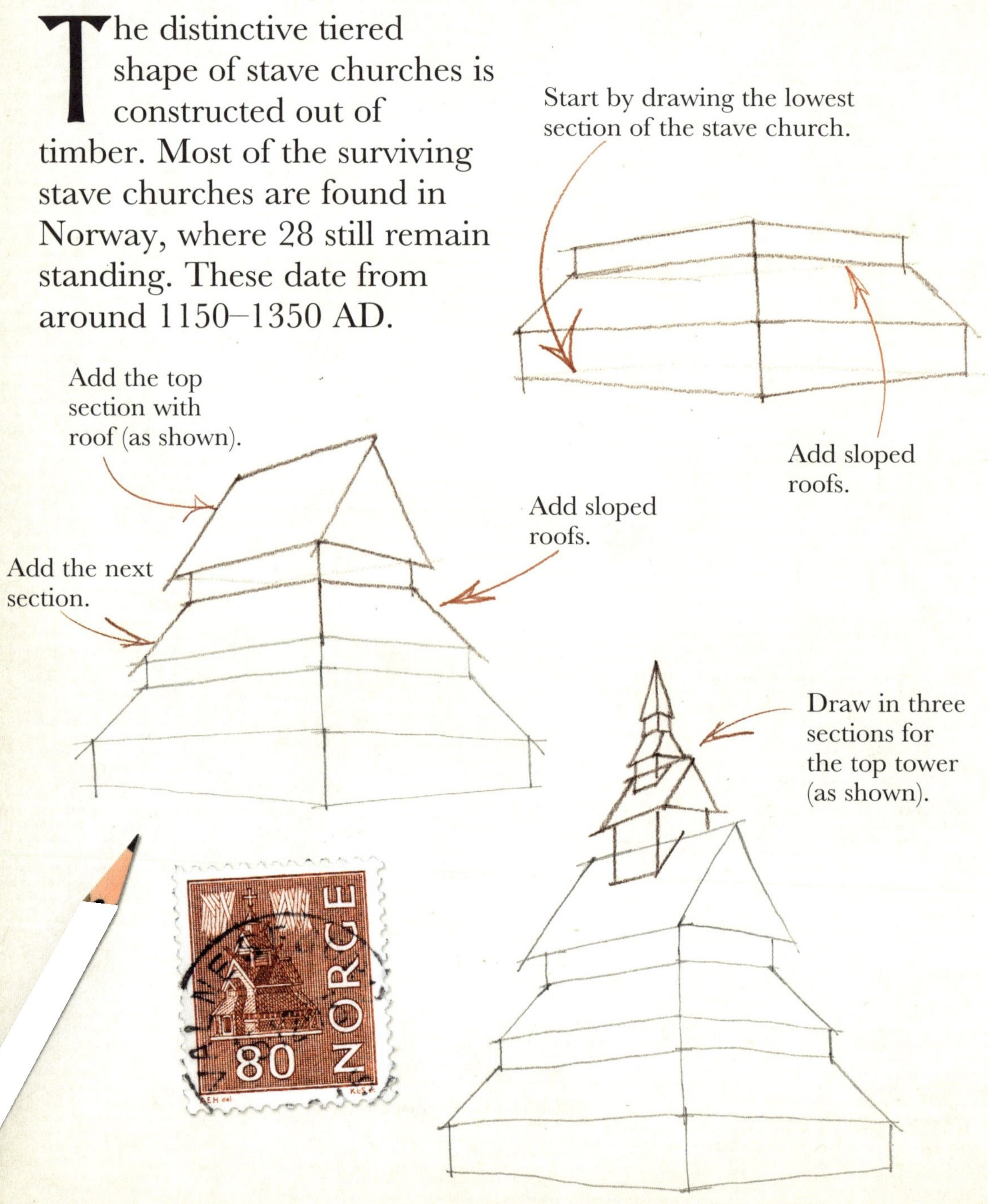

Add the roofed doorways (as shown).
Add all architectural details.
Add shading where light does not reach.
This close-up shows details of the carved dragons on the roof gables.
Add lines to show wooden stave construction.
Draw in guidelines to add roof shingles.
Finish all remaining details.
Add shading.
Add shading to the ground.
Erase any unwanted construction lines.

GLOSSARY

Amulet A piece of jewellery believed to have magical properties that would protect the possessor.

Caulking Sealing any gaps in the hull of a ship in order to make it watertight.

Chainmail Armour made of small metal rings that have been stuck together.

Clinker-built A method of building the hull of a ship where the planks of wood overlap each other.

Flax A crop that can be cultivated to produce textiles that can be used in the production of linen.

Fleece The wool on a sheep which can be used to make warm materials for clothing.

Goblet A drinking vessel, made of glass or metal, with a base but no handles.

Hierarchy A system where individuals or groups are ranked in order of their power and status.

Hull The body of a ship, including its sides and bottom.

Lye An alkaline solution used for washing and cleaning.

Memorial A monument established in order to remind people of an individual or important event.

Ornamentation Adding decorative elements to an item or building.

Pagans People who hold religious or spiritual beliefs different to the beliefs of the major world religions. Pagan religions often feature many gods instead of one all-powerful deity.

Peat A brown substance formed of decomposed vegetation dug up from out of the ground.

Piracy The criminal activity of boarding ships at sea and stealing their goods, often involving the threat of violence.

Prow The pointed front part of a ship.

Rudder A structure extending vertically into the water from the stern of a boat, used to steer the vessel.

Scandinavian Relating to the countries of Scandinavia – Norway, Denmark and Sweden – and their peoples and cultures.

Slav A person from one of the cultures in central and eastern Europe that speak Slavic languages.

Stern The rear part of a ship.

Thatch A roof covering made of materials like straw and reeds weaved together.

Watercolours Paints that can be mixed with water instead of oil.

INDEX